Bluegrass Guitar

Bluegrass Guitar

by Happy Traum

Oak Publications, New York
Music Sales Limited, London

I'd like to thank my friends Jim Rooney, Bill Keith, Eric Weissberg, and Jerry Tenney for their kind advice and the use of their extensive bluegrass record collections; and Russ Barenberg, Jon Sholle, David Nichtern, and Artie Traum for providing me with transcriptions of their fine guitar solos.

This book is lovingly dedicated to Jane, Merry, April, and Adam.

H.T.

Book design by Iris Weinstein and Mark Stein

PHOTOGRAPHS:

Kathy Butterfield:	page 118
Diana Davies:	page 13
Courtesy of Tom Delmore and Margaret Lindsay:	page 15 *(top)*
David Gahr:	pages 11, 29, 41, 57, 69, 70, 76, 93, 105, 112
Don Kissil:	pages 7, 19, 31, 47, 54, 61, 63, 74, 100, 113
Eric Levenson:	page 15 *(bottom)*
Jim McGuire-*Muleskinner News:*	page 35
Herb Wise:	cover, page 99 *(right)*
Unknown:	pages 44, 99 *(left)*

©1974 Oak Publications
A Division of Embassy Music Corporation
33 West 60th Street, New York 10023

Music Sales Limited
78 Newman Street, W1 London

Music Sales (Pty) Limited
27 Clarendon Street, Artarmon, Sydney NSW, Australia

International Standard Book Number 0-8256-0153-3
Library of Congress Catalogue Card Number 74-77312

Contents

(cont'd)

Parking lot picking - Don Reno

Introduction

When we think about bluegrass music, it is usually the technical virtuosity involved in playing it that first comes to mind; the leaping fiddle breaks, the streams of banjo notes, the piercing tones of the mandolin, the high, tight harmonies of the singers. That's all exciting, and gets cheers from the crowds, but it's not the whole story. As Bill Monroe has said:

> "It don't only take the fiddle or the banjo; the guitar man,
> he's got to learn too. It's a style. A guitar means as much in a
> bluegrass band as anything else. It just takes a lot of learning
> and a lot of practice."*

As most bluegrass musicians will tell you, the guitar is the backbone of a bluegrass band. Its traditional function is to provide a solid rhythmic background for the vocals, or against which the lead instruments can solo. The guitar is the middle-range instrument, filling out the sound of the group between the high lead notes and the bass, when there is one. (In some bands, the guitar takes over the function of the bass as well.) It is therefore essential that the guitarist develops a strong technique and a secure sense of time, since the others in the group will rely on him to hold it all together.

Aside from its function as a back-up instrument, the guitar has recently been thrust into the spotlight by an increasing number of flatpick virtuosi whose lightning fast licks and inventive solos have given the guitar new prominence in the world of bluegrass.

This book is meant to have three distinct purposes: It is an anthology of some of the best loved and most widely sung traditional bluegrass songs and instrumentals; it is a basic instruction method for novice guitarists who like bluegrass and want to play and sing it; and it is an advanced study book for those who would like to learn to play lead guitar solos in the styles of the great bluegrass flatpickers. Moreover, I have tried to document the dominant bluegrass guitar styles from the early "pre-bluegrass" old-time string band music to the present day "newgrass" picking of the younger soloists.

So, the way this book is used will depend on what you'd like to get out of it. It can be used simply as a songbook, and as such I would suggest that you leaf through it, picking out the songs you'd like to play, and using the chords provided to accompany yourself. If you are unfamiliar with a song, pick out the tune on your guitar or piano, then have a good time with it.

If you are learning to play guitar and are just getting into the bluegrass style, try playing the accompaniments written out in TAB under the melody line of the song. You'll probably find that there are bass runs, licks, rhythm changes, etc. that you have never done before, and that will increase your understanding of both the guitar and the bluegrass style of playing. Third, if you are a pretty accomplished back-up picker, but would like to learn lead instrumentals, try picking out the solos that I have written out. You'll find that they entail varying degrees of technical difficulty, but you will learn something from the simplest as well as those with the trickiest runs and licks. It is often the case that the most beautiful and rewarding musical passages are the sparest and most simple. Of course, there is always a great feeling of pride and accomplishment in executing a particularly difficult and flashy break with apparent ease. All it takes is patience and persistence.

*Bossmen: Bill Monroe & Muddy Waters, by James Rooney, Dial Press, N.Y.

A word about style: Like any traditional musical form, bluegrass has its distinct peculiarities of rhythm, accent, inflection, and intonation, which are impossible to impart via the printed page. It is necessary for anyone learning to play bluegrass (or blues, rock or Arabic folksongs) to engulf himself in the music *as played by* authentic bluegrass musicians. This entails listening to records and, where possible, hearing musicians play in person at festivals, concerts, night clubs, and parties. Listen and feel for the accents, the placement of the runs, slides, chord positions, etc. There is no substitute for hearing it done right to enable you to get into the style.

It is even more important to play with others who are into bluegrass and develop your sense of participation in a band situation. This means learning to hear all the subtleties of four or five instruments playing together, blending voices in bluegrass harmonies, and even moving comfortably around a microphone. This doesn't mean that you've got to become a professional musician, but bluegrass is a group endeavor, so it's important to interact with other musicians in any way you can. Bluegrass clubs, parties, and "parking lot jam sessions" at festivals are good ways to make contact with other pickers, and playing with them can be the start of a long and fruitful relationship. One of the nice things about playing bluegrass is that there is a standard repertoire, so you can go to a festival and jam with folks you've never met before and have no trouble finding material that you both know. (Try going to a bluegrass festival and see if you can find someone who *can't* play "Footprints in the Snow" or "Under the Double Eagle".)

As you play the songs in this book, try to listen to the record of the particular performance that has been transcribed, or if that is not available, one by another group. (It may be difficult to find many of the records in your local store, but you may find them through bluegrass clubs, newsletters, tape exchanges, or from mail order houses. See appendix for more details.) Play right along with the records—it will be a big help in getting your chops together.

When you learn a new solo or back-up part from this book, try it out with some friends. If you have a choice in the matter, always try to play with someone a little better than you. As you'll know if you are into athletics, it is good to have to push a little to keep up. If you see a friend playing a chord position or a run that is unfamiliar, get him aside after the session to show it to you. Chances are, he learned it the same way from someone a little better than him.

The songs and instrumentals as written in this book should not be considered the final version and the only way to play them. All good music is improvisational, and it is important not to get stuck only with what's been written down. The person whose solo I have transcribed will probably never play that solo exactly the same way again, but the recording machine happened to catch one of an infinite variety of notes. The fact that it is written down in this book is only an accident of history, so be free with your own music, within the confines of the bluegrass style. Your music will be much better for it.

As soon as you are familiar with a song, or have the general idea of a back-up or solo part, take it from there, referring back to the printed music for new ideas or to keep yourself on the right track. This way you will eventually develop your own style, and will be expressing yourself in your own distinctive way. That is the point at which any musician becomes a creative artist, regardless of the musical form he is using as the vehicle for his self expression.

A brief history of the guitar in bluegrass music

Bluegrass music is a direct descendant of the old-time string band tradition, which in turn developed out of southern mountain dance music and songs. The southern mountains have been a vast repository of traditional music since the 17th century when the hills were first settled by English, Scottish, and Irish immigrants who brought with them their incredibly rich ballad and song tradition. Isolated in the hills for generations, the music flourished almost unchanged until the early part of this century when the mountains became accessible to outside influence, making possible an exchange of musical (and other) ideas. Mountain music held on and grew despite the pressures from more socially acceptable forms of popular music, and although some change did occur, the rural people of the south and other parts of the country clung tenaciously to the music which has become one of the most valuable contributions to American culture.

When it finally emerged from its isolation, the music took on a new character. The Black music of the rural south was the other powerfully influential cultural development, with its blues shouters, guitar pickers, jug bands, minstrel shows, and of course, the new jazz combos of the day. It was at least partly through this influence that the primarily unaccompanied vocal music started to take on the instrumental qualities as we know them today.

Of course, the fiddle and banjo had been used as the basic dance band instruments for years (when allowed by the religious mores of the area) but the guitar only appeared in the 1920's as a backup instrument, providing the rhythm behind the lead instruments or an accompaniment for a singer.

The bluegrass guitar style started to emerge with the first commercial performances of old-time instrumental music. Groups and individual artists such as J.E. Mainer and his Mountaineers, Gid Tanner and The Skillet Lickers, Charlie Poole, The Carter Family, Jimmie Rodgers, and The Delmore Brothers, are all good examples of what is essentially the same style of guitar playing that we know so well today. There are many records available of these early country musicians in which the simple boom-chicka boom-chicka rhythm and strong bass runs can be clearly heard. The style is simple and direct, but perfectly suited to the straight-forward music it accompanies.

Lead guitar on these early recordings was rare, although Maybelle Carter's powerful melody picking (her thumb played lead while her index finger filled out the rhythm in the treble) did a great deal to inspire more ambitious guitar pickers and push the guitar into the foreground. Alton Delmore of the Delmore Brothers was another example of an early lead guitarist, and almost all of their songs features his simple but powerful flat picking solos, played against Rabon's tenor guitar rhythm. These examples are the exception rather than the rule, though, and most country music guitarists were content to back up the other lead instruments, especially fiddle, mandolin and banjo.

The term "bluegrass", which incidentally did not come into popular usage until the early '50s, was originally used to describe a new kind of country string band music developed by Bill Monroe in the late '30s. Monroe, who for years has been called "The Daddy of Bluegrass", comes from Kentucky (The Blue Grass State) and chose that name for his band, The Blue Grass Boys. Bill Monroe's main instrument, of course, is the mandolin (for which he has developed a distinctive and very influential style), but he has always played with a guitar back-up. His earliest recordings were with his brother Charlie, and The Monroe Brothers, like other country groups, sang tight harmonies with Bill's mandolin taking the instrumental solos and Charlie's guitar keeping the solid rhythm chords and bass lines going behind him. It was Bill's high mountain tenor, though, that was so captivating about their sound. Often called "the high, lonesome sound" when describing the mountain balladeers, Bill Monroe's singing was directly influenced by the mountain church singing and modal harmonies of his youth in western Kentucky. (For comparison, listen to recordings of old time ballad singers such as Roscoe Holcomb, Horton Barker, and Clarence Ashley.) The "high lonesome sound" is also especially prevalent in the bluegrass music of The Stanley Brothers, Ralph and Carter, from the Clinch Mountain region of Virginia.

It was in the late 1940's that Bill Monroe started to break away from the old-time music and formed the bluegrass sound that had such an explosive influence on the country music scene. His new group featured a young Earl Scruggs on 5-string banjo, and the unusually complex three-finger picking, combined with Monroe's driving mandolin, Lester Flatt's guitar, and Chubby Wise's fiddle, gave the group a power and excitement not heard before in country music. This was the group that was to be the model for all bluegrass groups to come.

By the mid-50s there were several highly professional bluegrass bands travelling the country, recording, and playing on radio programs such as Nashville's Grand Ol' Opry and WWVA's Jamboree from Wheeling, West Virginia. Included in these groups were many musicians who had served a brief but important apprenticeship with Bill Monroe, notably Flatt and Scruggs, Jimmy Martin, Carter Stanley, Don Reno, Mac Wiseman, and Sonny Osborn to name a few of the men who started carving a permanent name for bluegrass music in the annals of American popular culture.

For the most part, bluegrass guitarists still kept pretty much in the background, punching out the rhythm and interspersing bass runs with a few licks, such as Lester Flatt's famous "G run" that's been played by every bluegrass guitarist in the world. Two notable exceptions are the lead guitar playing of George Shuffler on The Stanley Brothers early albums,

Sara and Maybelle Carter

13

and Don Reno, best known as a banjo picker but an excellent flatpicker as well. Both of these men brought a new sophistication and technical expertise to bluegrass guitar playing. Still, as I have said, the guitarist was the indispensible mainstay of the bluegrass band, and Lester Flatt, Charlie Monroe, Red Smiley, Carter Stanley, Charlie Waller, Jimmy Martin, and dozens of other guitar pickers and singers filled the role well.

It was not until the sixties that the guitar really came into its own as a lead instrument worthy of a solo in a bluegrass instrumental or song. The most dynamic guitarist to emerge from the country music scene was not a bluegrass musician at all, but a mountain singer from North Carolina named Doc Watson. Doc, of course, was proficient in nearly every musical field, but it was as a traditional folk musician that he found his first large audiences. He knew hundreds of songs and sang them in a rich, dark baritone voice while picking the guitar and banjo, or blowing his mouth harp, but when he launched into one of his incomparably flatpicked fiddle tunes he just about blew everyone out of the room. His influence was immediate, and the youngsters all over America started learning to play lead acoustic guitar with a flatpick.

One of those who picked up on Doc's style was a young man named Clarence White, who first came to prominence in a bluegrass group called The Kentucky Colonels. Clarence added a more contemporary feeling to the style, and reworked Doc's cross-picking techniques into his own musical trademark. Clarence went on to work as lead guitarist with The Byrds and played on numerous recording sessions. At the time of his tragic death in 1973 he was already considered to be one of the greatest country guitarists ever.

Thanks to the influence of men like Doc Watson, Clarence White, George Shuffler, Don Reno and others, many more guitarists have followed and developed their own lead guitar techniques—Dan Crary, John Herald, Norman Blake, David Bromberg, and Russ Barenberg among them. In the pages that follow I have tried to set down a fairly representative cross section of bluegrass guitar playing, from the simplest back-up strums to the most advanced examples of "newgrass" picking that I could find. My book is by no means complete, since it would be almost impossible to mention everyone and notate all the songs that brought us up to this musical point. It is my hope though, that you will take what you learn here and explore and experiment for yourself, finding new and old songs and joining these ranks of fine bluegrass musicians.

The Delmore Brothers

Don Reno and Red Smiley

Playing bluegrass guitar

If you are a beginning guitarist, the first thing you'll have to do is become familiar with the basic chords. Since most bluegrass guitarists use the open position chords, you need only be familiar with a handful (!) to play most of the songs in this book. These chords, though, are your basic musical vocabulary, and it is essential that you are able to move freely and quickly from one to the other. Use the following diagrams as a check-list of chords you will need to know.

Basic chords

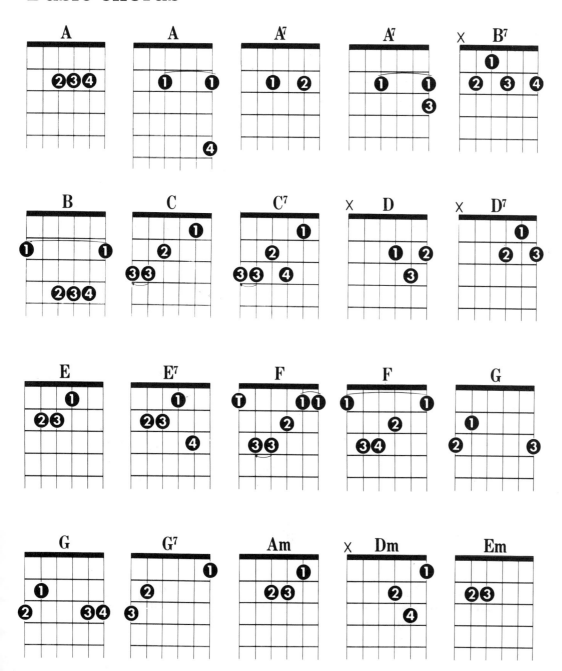

The pick

Although some guitarists play bluegrass finger style (Maybelle Carter, Lester Flatt, Red Smiley) the large majority of bluegrass pickers play with a flat pick. If you are not already acquainted with its use, get ahold of one and start practicing with it. Here is some information to help you get started.

A flat pick (or plectrum) can be made of a number of materials—I've seen them in felt, wood, metal, bone, hard nylon and tortoise shell (the best, in my opinion)—but in this country most are made of plastic (cheapest and longest lasting). The most common type is triangular, about 1" to a side, but some are almost round, some long and skinny, some S-shaped, and so on. They also come in varying degrees of thickness, from paper-thin to fairly hard and inflexible. The only way to find out which to use is to try them all and see which feels best. If you are playing a lot of fast single-string work on the treble strings, you might want a thin, light pick, but if you are into heavy rhythm and bass work you will want something harder. For myself, I like to use a medium gauge pick, but I try to find one a little on the thin side for more flexibility.

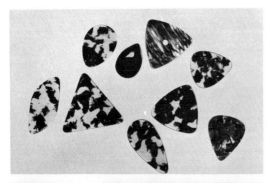

The pick is held between the thumb and forefinger, but not gripped too tightly. Although there are as many ways of holding the pick as there are pickers, the most usual way to start is: Hold your right hand in a relaxed way so that your fingers are curled half-way between open and closed. Lay your thumb gently on the side of your index finger so that the outside edge of your first thumb joint is about even with the first joint of your index finger. Your other three fingers should be relaxed, not clenched in a fist. Now slide your pick between your thumb and index finger with the point perpendicular to your index finger nail. How much of the point you want sticking past your finger will be up to you, and as you experiment you'll find the right position.

The pick should strike the string as perpendicular as possible. It will take a good deal of practice before you get sharp, clean notes and easy-sounding chords, so don't get discouraged. Try to control the pick so you aren't playing too loudly. When you are strumming a chord, the pick should brush the strings gently but evenly.

Here is a hint that might help you with that pick control. Many guitarists (myself included) use their right pinky resting lightly on the pick guard (the plastic thing under the sound hole) to guide their hand while picking. Many finger pickers use this technique also, although classical guitarists frown on the practice. Among those who use it, some anchor their finger in one place, but for flat-picking I prefer letting it glide easily over the pick guard with just enough pressure to let you feel where your hand is in relation to the strings. After a while most people fall into their own hand patterns, but in the meantime I think this will help.

Lester Flatt and the Nashville Grass

Reading tablature

The guitar tablature provided here is a substitute for (or a supplement to) the standard musical notation. The six lines represent the six strings of the guitar, with the bass E as the bottom line.

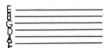

The number on the line is the fret at which the left hand finger stops the string. Thus, a C chord would be shown as

Two notes tied together with the letter "h" in between indicates a "hammer-on":

"p" is a "pull-off" (left hand pluck):

"s" is a slide from one fret to another, or to a fret from an optional point below it:

Pick direction is indicated as follows:

⊓   = downstroke

V   = upstroke

Basic picking

The basic strum in bluegrass music is the same one that has been found throughout American country music, the one I have called The Country Lick. This is the *boom-chicka* rhythm—a cleanly picked bass note followed by a down-up combination on the treble strings. The strum is written out this way in music and TAB:

Waltz (3/4) time is slightly different: boom-chicka-chicka, boom-chicka-chicka:

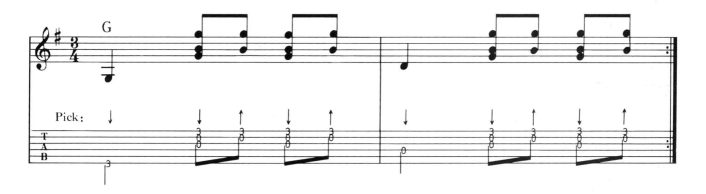

Although the strummed part of the lick is precisely notated, in actual playing your pick will brush across two, three, or four strings, depending on your personal touch and the sound you want. I have consistently written it a certain way (the down stroke ↓ playing three strings, the up stroke ↑ two) to approximate the way it will *usually* be played. Please don't be too concerned with hitting the exact strings I have notated, but concentrate on getting the motion right. The bass notes, however, must be precise.

By changing chords in the standard bluegrass progression, you will begin to see the bass notes forming a pattern of their own. The bass notes you choose will be very important to the sound you are trying to achieve, so pay special attention to them. For example, here is the basic three-chord progression in G. Play it and you will hear the bass note progression.

For the sake of simplicity and clarity, I have not put in pick direction after this, except where absolutely necessary. Therefore, it would be useful to follow this rule: *Down* (↓) on a strong beat, *Up* (↑) on a weak beat.

When playing the standard country lick, then, your pick strokes will look like this:

The bass notes will generally be picked in a downward motion, except when you are picking a fast run. Then you will alternate between down and up strokes:

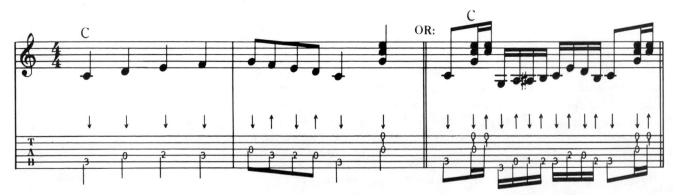

In Certain songs you might want to add a little oomph to the rhythm of your strum by adding an extra up-stroke between the bass note and the first down stroke, changing the rhythm sound to *boompa*-chicka, *boompa*-chicha:

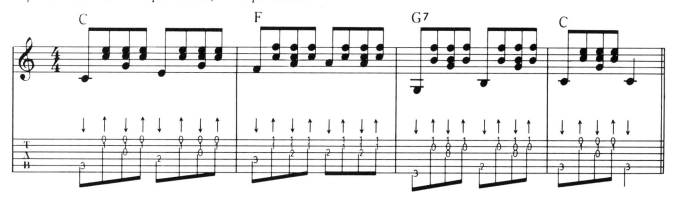

You'll have to practice this until it comes smooth and easy without it sounding too harsh or frantic. Make sure your bass notes are always sharp and clear.

After playing these strums for a while, and listening to the bass note patterns, you may also notice that certain bass notes closely resemble the melody of the song you are playing. Pay attention when this occurs, because it will eventually form the basis for one style of melody picking. Often called "Carter Family Picking" after Maybelle's great style, the melody is played on the bass notes while the rhythm strumming continues on the treble strings. As you'll see, many of the songs that follow have breaks in this style.

Hammering and pulling

When playing an accompaniment or a melody, a little interest can be added by using some well-placed hammer-ons and pull-offs. With both of these techniques, the idea is to change the pitch of a note without plucking it again with your right hand.

With the hammer-on, you pick the string and while it is ringing you bring a finger of your left hand down on a given fred hard enough so that it keeps vibrating, changing the pitch of the original note.

A pull-off is pretty much the same thing in reverse, plucking the string with the left hand finger that is fretting it:

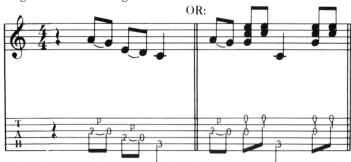

When hammering-on or pulling-off, the basic rhythm of your country lick doesn't change. The extra note just sneaks right in between the picked bass note and the down strum:

Chords can flow from one to the other by the use of bass runs, which are used to break up the monotony of the constant strum, and sometimes provides a harmony line to the melody of the song. I won't illustrate the bass run here, since they occur in just about every bluegrass back-up arrangement in the book. Just watch for it.

The G run

As I mentioned earlier, the most famous bluegrass guitar run is the one known as the "Flatt" or "G" run (since it is almost always played in the key of G). Over the years, it has become the cliche of bluegrass guitar picking, and it is used to end breaks, begin them, accent a phrase, or even end a line of music. It is so important that I'm going to give it to you here, so if you are not already familiar with it you can practice it and be ready when you want to throw it into a song. It can be played in several ways—here are a few:

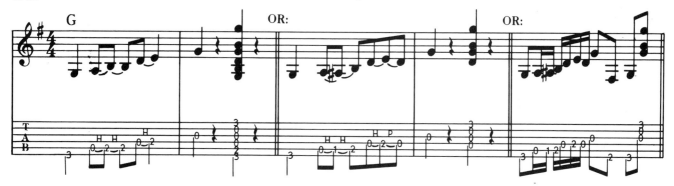

Despite its name, this run can and should be played in all the basic keys, so here it is in C, D, A, and E:

As you are learning this, listen for it in bluegrass songs on records. After a while it will be unmistakable, and you will even be able to anticipate the run before you have heard the song through. You'll find this run scattered throughout the arrangements in this book. Sometimes it will be just three or four notes, and sometimes the full run, but it will always be used to accent and give extra punch to a song or phrase. Use it well.

Intros and endings

Of course, there are other runs in bluegrass as well. The most popular, after the "G run", is the old "Shave and a haircut—shampoo".

No one plays it that straight, though, so it's important for you to be able to improvise your own runs based on that figure. These figures are usually used as endings to songs or instrumentals, but can also be used to start one off. Here's the way you might transform the simple "Shave and a haircut" into a more complex riff.

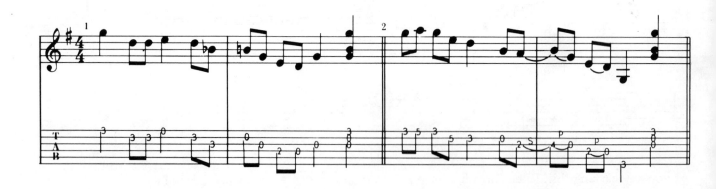

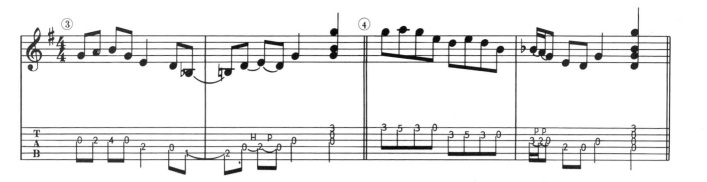

Now here are some similar runs in other keys. Once you are familiar with them, try using them as the basis for a complete solo, rather than just a brief run.

28

In the following pages there will be other runs as well, but I'll let you discover them yourself. The lead arrangements are, I think, self explanatory, but when we come to new techniques or special problems I'll bring them to your attention. Meanwhile, play and sing the following songs, and, above all, enjoy them. Then try to get together with some friends playing banjo, mandolin, fiddle, or another guitar, and try to put what you have learned here into a group effort. Then it should all fall into place, and you'll be a bluegrass guitarist.

Good luck!
Happy Traum

Happy Traum

Bluegrass songs

Del McCoury and Group

Mama Don't 'Low

This is *the* traditional bluegrass mob scene jamming song. A band with good instrumental-ists can use this as a novelty number to show off each member's talents, and it's usually a show-stopper. I used to play this at parties and in Washington Square, New York's meet-ing place for folk and bluegrass pickers. Each person in the group takes a solo after the chorus in which his instrument is sung about. (Mama don't 'low no banjo picking 'round here; fiddle playing; dobro playing; washtub thumping; harmonica blowing; clog dancing; etc.)

I've written out two guitar solos. The first is based rather heavily on the "G run", and the second makes more use of the treble strings and is more the way I might play it myself. Both are valuable for developing fast runs and accurate pick technique.

ma-ma don't 'low no guit - ar pick-in' round   here.

Instrumental 1

Charlie Monroe

New River Train

This is one of those old songs for which you can make up verses as you go along. I've never heard it sung the same way twice.

The Monroe Brothers recorded a spirited version back in the thirties, and I've transcribed Charlie Monroe's guitar back-up, which is simple but effective. This will be especially good for you to learn if you are just starting out with your guitar playing.
I've also written out three different instrumentals, to try and show you how you can build solos in this style. The first is pretty much the bare melody and very similar to Charlie's back-up part. In the variations that follow, I have added more runs until, in the third solo, there are practically no rhythm chords. Practice this with someone else keeping time on a second guitar or other instrument, and try to get the alternate picking clean and at an even tempo. Start slowly if necessary, building up your speed.

I've added some arrows here and there to remind you of your pick direction. Remember: the pick comes down on the strong beat, up on the weak beat.

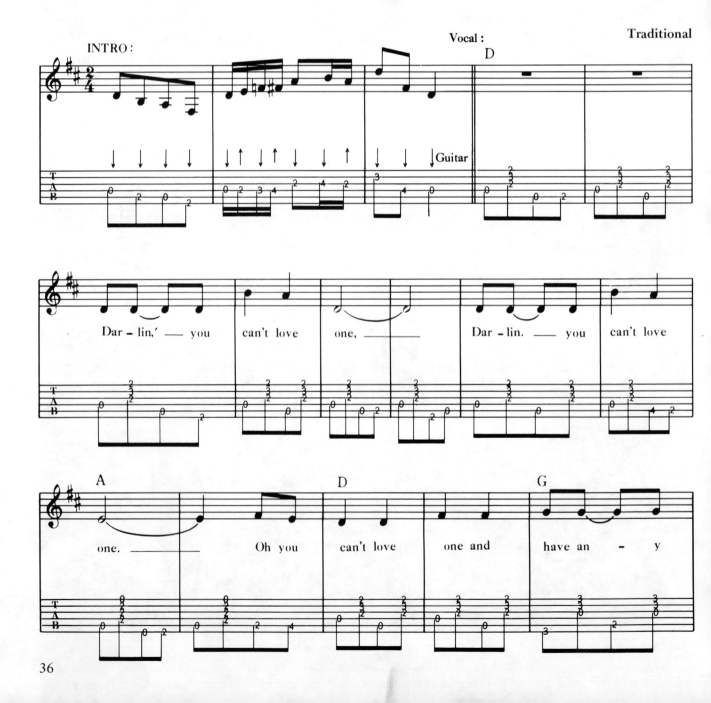

36

Chorus:

Riding on that new river train
Riding on that new river train
Same old train that brought me here
And it's gonna carry me away.

Darling you can't love two
Darling you can't love two
You can't love two
And your little heart be true
No darling you can't love two.

Chorus:

Darling you can't love three
Darling you can't love three
You can't love three
And still love me
Darling you can't love three.

Chorus:

Darling you can't love four
Darling you can't love four
You can't love four
And love me anymore
Darling you can't love four.

Chorus:

Darling you can't love five
Darling you can't love five
You can't love five
And get honey from my beehive
Darling you can't love five.

Chorus:

Darling you can't love six
Darling you can't love six
You can't love six
That kind of love won't mix
Darling you can't love six.

Chorus:

39

Roll In My Sweet Baby's Arms

Another old-time bluegrass classic, made popular by Flatt and Scruggs but performed by dozens of bluegrass groups over the years. It was recently made into a pop-country hit (with some good banjo picking) by Leon (Hank Wilson) Russell. An excellent version of it can also be heard on Del McCoury's Arhoolie album (F 5006). The back-up part I have written out is similar to his. On the verse section, I have illustrated the use of rhythm "chops" in which you fret a closed chord and damp the strings immediately after striking them with the pick. These chords are played on the off-beat (back-beat), and are usually played by the banjo, although the guitarist often does it as well. It's a good thing to have in your bag in case you need it.

The instrumental break is my own, and it should give you something to work on. Don't forget to alternate your pick strokes on the fast (sixteenth) notes.

Earl Scruggs, Lester Flatt and the Foggy Mountain Boys

Roll In My Sweet Baby's Arms

Traditional

Roll in ___ my sweet ba - by's arms. Roll in ___ my sweet ba - by's arms.

Lay'round this shack' til the mail train-comes back and roll in my sweet ba - by's arms.

Ain't gon - na work on ___ the rail - road, Ain't gon - na work on ___ the farm,

Lay ' round ___ this shack til the mail-train comes back and roll in ___ my sweet ba - by's arms.

Chorus:

Now where was you last Friday night
While I was laying in jail
Walking the streets with another man
Wouldn't even go my bail.

Chorus:

I know your parents don't like me
Drove me away from your door
If I had my life to live over
I'd never go there anymore.

Chorus:

Repeat chorus:

Bury Me Beneath The Willow

This arrangement was taken from a fine version of this traditional bluegrass classic by The Stanley Brothers. Both the introduction and back-up part were probably played by George Shuffler. Some of his runs might be difficult to play while singing the song, but I put them in as a fine example of the use of more complicated runs in back-up playing. Notice that many of the up-strokes in the instrumental section pick just the single first string, rather than a chord.

From *The Stanley Brothers Sing Everybody's Country Favorites*, King 690.

Ralph Stanley and George Shuffler

Bury Me Beneath The Willow

wil - low, un - der the weep - in wil - low tree,

So he may

know where I am sleep - in,

Then per - haps he'll weep for me.

My heart is sad and I am lonely
For the only one I love
When shall I see him, oh no never
'Til we meet in heaven above.

Chorus:

Go bury me beneath the willow
Under the weeping willow tree
So he may know where I am sleepin'
Then perhaps he'll think of me.

Chorus:

He told me that he dearly love me
How could I believe it untrue
Until the angel softly whispered
He will prove untrue to you.

Chorus:

Tomorrow was our wedding day
Oh God, oh God, where is he
He's over talking to another
And now he cares no more for me.

Chorus:

Going to Georgia

This is a combination of two versions. The accompaniment under the melody is based on Wade Mainer and Zeke Morris' exuberant performance, recorded in 1936 in North Carolina and reissued on RCA's *Early Blue Grass* (LPV-569), part of their great "Vintage Series". Wade Mainer, who played banjo and harmonica on this cut, was the leader of Mainer's Mountaineers. Zeke Morris, who played the guitar, was one half of the Morris Brothers. He and Wiley Morris wrote and sang many great songs, including the classic "Salty Dog Blues".

The instrumental break was taken from a more recent bluegrass-style performance of the song by Ralph Stanley on an album called *Something Old—Something New* (Rebel SLP-1503). Keith Whitley, the lead guitarist on the album, plays a nice solo in which his "boom-chicka" strum is played on the single melody string, sounding almost like a rhythmic tremelo. I've written out two of his variations.

"Going to Georgia" is a lively, dance tune version of the well-known "Rye Whiskey".

Keith Whitley

Going to Georgia

Traditional

I'm go-ing to Geor-gia, I'm go-ing to stay, I'm go-ing to Geor-gia, to wor-ry my life a-way.

I once loved a young man
As dear as my life
Oftimes he promised
To make me his wife,

He fulfulled his promise
To make me his wife
You see what I've come to
From being his wife.

My foot's in my chair
My life's in my hand
I'm courtin' you darlin'
To marry you if I can.

I'm going to Georgia
I'm going to roam
I'm going to Georgia
To make it my home.

My children are hungry
I'm sick in my bed
My husband's a drunkard,
I wish I were dead.

Instrumental

Handsome Molly

This old mountain ballad has always been a favorite of mine. You can hear it sung and played by The Country Gentlemen (Folkways FA 2410) in bluegrass style, and by *Borderline*, a country-rock group with Jim Rooney (United Artists AV-LA016-F).

Traditional

Chorus:

Chorus:

Sailing around the ocean
Sailing around the sea
I think of handsome Molly
Wherever she may be.

Her hair was black as a raven's
Her eyes were bright as coals
Her teeth shone like lilies
Out in the morning cold.

Chorus:

Oh don't you remember Molly
When you give me your right hand
You said if you ever marry
That I would be your man.

I saw her in church last Sunday
She passed me on by
I knew her mind was changing
By the roving of her eye.

Chorus:

Repeat first verse:

Chorus:

Instrumental

You're A Flower In The Wildwood

Del McCoury is a solid bluegrass flatpicker with a strong, almost piercing tenor voice. This version is from his album *Del McCoury Sings Bluegrass* (Arhoolie F 5006). As you can see, Del likes to use the "G run" quite a bit.

Another performance of this song can be heard by Bill Harrell and The Virginians *(The Wonderful World of Bluegrass*—United Artists UAL 3293).

flow - er bloom-in' there for me, Sweet-er than the morn-ing dew, and I'll

soon re - turn to you you're a flow'r that is bloom-ing there for me.

Then this message came to me
From the captain on the sea
And it told me that my darlin' was dead

Oh the shocking words surprised
Brought the teardrops to my eyes
When I thought about the last words that I said

Chorus:

Now he can't return to me
He got drowned in the sea
And he's past over life's weary way

When it's in the month of June
And the roses are in bloom
Oh it seems that I can hear my darling say

Chorus:

Del McCoury

Old Rattler

The Stanley Brothers have always been a favorite group of mine. Their singing has remained firmly in its Virginia mountain roots, and has never lost the mournful inflection or subtle ornamentation of the best southern mountain vocal music. Just listen to Carter Stanley's powerful "I Am A Man Of Constant Sorrow" and you'll understand what I mean.

"Old Rattler" is another traditional song, and the group's rich harmonies on the chorus brings to mind the song's probable origin in England. In fact, if you close your eyes and try to block out the instruments, you can almost hear an English group like The Watersons or The Young Tradition doing the song.

The instrumentals are fine, though, especially George Shufflers fast flatpicking trading off with Ralph Stanley's banjo. Shuffler capos way up the neck to give his guitar a bright, high sound, and strums hard and fast, picking out precise bass notes. Start out slow and build up your speed gradually. Listen to and play along with the record: *The Stanley Brothers Sing Everybody's Country Favorites,* (King 690).

Original Key: B♭
Capo 10 Fret

Traditional

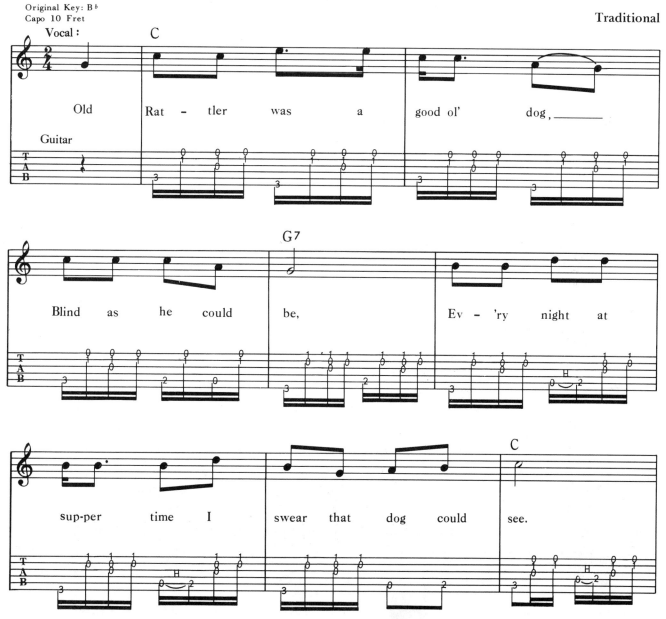

Old Rattler treed the other night
I thought he treed a coon
When I come to find it out
He was barkin' at the moon.

Chorus:

Grandma had a yellow hen
Who set her as you know
Set her on three buzzard eggs
And hatched out Grandpa Jones.

Chorus:

Grandma had a mulie cow
Mulie when she's born
Took a jaybird forty years
To fly from horn to horn.

Chorus:

Stanley Brothers with George Shuffler

Midnight On The Stormy Deep

This traditional ballad was recorded by Bill Monroe in 1966, a time that he was using many young city-bred bluegrass musicians, such as Bill Keith, banjo; Richard Greene, fiddle; and Peter Rowan, guitar. All of these men later went on to play other forms of music, but benefitted greatly by their work with Monroe.

The accompaniment on this song was taken from the playing of Peter Rowan (who also sang lead to Monroe's high harmony) on *Blue Grass Time* (Decca DL 74896).

58

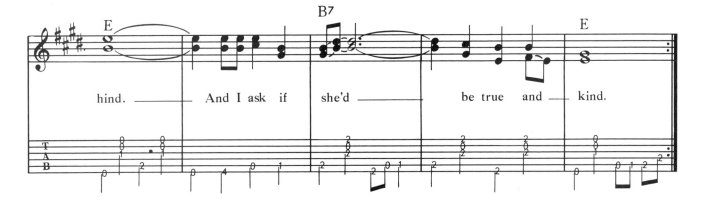

hind. _____ And I ask if she'd _____ be true and _____ kind.

I never shall forget the day
That I was forced to go away
In silence there my head she'd rest
And press me to her loving breast.

Oh Willy, don't go back to sea
There's other girls as good as me
But none can love you true as I
Pray don't go where the bullets fly.

The deep, deep sea may us divide
And I may be some other's bride
But still my thoughts will sometimes stray
To thee when thou art far away.

I never have proved false to thee
The heart I gave was true as thine
But you have proven untrue to me
I can no longer call thee mine.

Then fare thee well, I'd rather make
My home upon some icy lake
Where the southern sun refuse to shine
Than to trust a love so false as thine.

Rosa Lee McFall

The Monroe Brothers' relationship to old time mountain music was never more evident than in their performance of this traditional song. Charlie Monroe's guitar playing rippled throughout with his use of hammer-ons on almost every beat. Try to keep the strum and the melody notes flowing along at an even, smooth pace.

This can be heard on another fine reissue called *Early Blue Grass Music by The Monroe Brothers* (CAL-774), on RCA's Camden label.

Her eyes were bright and shiny
Her voice was sweet to me
I knew that I would always love her
I thought that she loved me.

I asked her to be my darlin'
And this is what she said
I know that I'll always be happy
When you and I are wed.

But God way up in heaven
For her one day did call
I lost my bride, oh how I loved her
My Rosa Lee McFall.

I'll roam this wide world over
Through cities great and small
Til God prepares my home in heaven
With my Rosa Lee McFall.

Bill Monroe with James Monroe, Richard Greene and Peter Rowan

Instrumental

I Am A Pilgrim

This old hymn was originally made famous by Merle Travis, whose recording of it on *Back Home* (Capitol T891) inspired a whole generation of guitar fingerpickers. About twenty years later, Clarence White and the Kentucky Colonels recorded it as an instrumental on their classic *Appalachian Swing!* album (World-Pacific 1821). I've taken Clarence's back-up part and put it under the song, so you can sing it and use Clarence's accompaniment. Then, if you are feeling confident, try the transcription of his solo. It's tricky, and it will really help if you can get hold of the record, so you can hear the subtleties that don't come across the printed page.

When Clarence White was killed last year in a tragic accident, the world lost one of its greatest country guitar pickers. His music will live on for many years to come, hopefully inspiring young guitarists to try and pick up where he left off.

Clarence White

I Am A Pilgrim

I have a father, and a mother,
sister and brother, gone on before.
Bye and bye I'm going to meet them, Oh God
where we'll dwell, forever more.

Well, I have trials and tribulations;
I have trouble on ev'ry hand.
But I've started for that city, Oh God
And, I'm doin' the best I can.

Angel Band

This is another one of those Gospel classics. This comes from Ralph Stanley's superb performance on *Country Pickin' and Singin'*, The Stanley Brothers and the Clinch Mountain Boys (Mercury MG 20349). Another fine version can be heard on *Songs of Glory*—Earl Scruggs and Lester Flatt (Columbia—CL 1424). Incidentally, Earl does some fine guitar picking on this album!

Chorus:

68

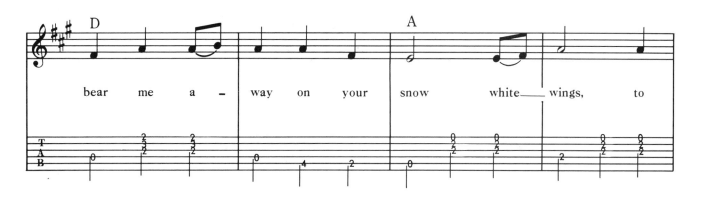

bear me a – way on your snow white—— wings, to

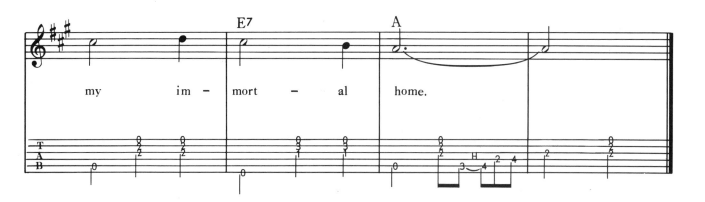

my im – mort – al home.

Oh bear my longing heart to Him
Who bled and died for me
Whose blood now cleanses from all sin
And gives me victory.

Chorus:

I know I'm near the holy ranks
Of friends and kindred dear
I've brushed the dew on Jordan's banks
The crossing must be near.

Chorus:

I've almost gained my Heavenly home
My spirit loudly sings
The Holy ones, behold they come
I hear the noise of wings.

Chorus:

Earl Scruggs, Lester Flatt and the Foggy Mountain Boys

Crying Holy

This wonderful old-time hymn has been recorded many times by bluegrass groups, but my favorites are a 1940 version by Bill Monroe and His Blue Grass Boys *(Early Bluegrass,* RCA LPV-569), and the old pre-bluegrass version by The Carter Family *(Great Sacred Songs*—Columbia/Harmony HL 7396).

Bill Monroe and Don Reno

Crying Holy

Vocal

Traditional

Sinners run   and hide your face
Sinners run   and hide your face
Go run into the rocks
And hide your face
Cause I ain't (Lord, Lord) no stranger now.

Chorus:

Lord I ain't   no stranger now
Lord I ain't   no stranger now
I've been introduced to the Father and the Son
And I ain't (Lord, Lord) no stranger now.

Chorus:

Instrumental

Standing In The Need Of Prayer

Another old Gospel song, from the singing of The Country Gentlemen (Folkways FA 2410). Charlie Waller plays a simple rhythm guitar part, adding a run for accent at the very end of each verse.

I made up an instrumental that will give you some practice moving up the neck. Don't forget to alternate your pick strokes on the eighth notes.

Traditional

Chorus:

It's me, it's me oh, Lord
Standing in the need of prayer
It's me, it's me oh, Lord
Standing in the need of prayer.

Not my papa, not my mother,
But it's me oh, Lord
Standing in the need of prayer
Not my papa, not my mother,
But it's me oh, Lord
Standing in the need of prayer.

Chorus:

Not the preacher, not the sinner,
But it's me oh, Lord
Standing in the need of prayer
Not the preacher, not the sinner,
But it's me oh, Lord
Standing in the need of prayer.

Chorus:

Charlie Waller and the Country Gentlemen

Instrumental

All The Good Times

This has been one of the most widely sung and best loved bluegrass songs since the Monroe Brothers recorded it in 1937. Charlie Monroe played the guitar accompaniment two different ways, depending on whether it was behind the vocal or the instrumental (mandolin and guitar) solo, so I've given it to you both ways. He plays it very simply when singing, and puts in many more bass runs when they are just playing.

This version is from the RCA Vintage Series reissue called *Early Blue Grass* (LPV-569). Bill Monroe also recorded it on *Blue Grass Time* (Decca DL 74896) with Peter Rowan playing guitar.

Bill Monroe

All The Good Times

Traditional

(Early Monroe Version)

I wish to the Lord I'd never been born
Or died when I was young
And never had seen your sparkling blue eyes
Or wherever your light did shine.

Chorus:

Come back, come back my own true love
And stay a while with me
For if ever I had a friend in this world
You been a friend to me.

Chorus:

Don't you see that distant train
Come whirling around the bend
It's taking me away from this old town
To never return again.

Chorus:

I wish to the Lord I'd never been born
Or died when I was young
I never would have seen your sparkling blue eyes
Or heard your lying tongue.

Chorus:

All the good times are past and gone
All the good times are o'er
All the good times are past and gone
Darling don't you weep for me.

Chorus:

See that lonesome turtle dove
Come flying from pine to pine
He's mourning for his own true love
Just like I mourn for mine.

Chorus:

Come back, come back my own true love
Come and stay a while with me
For if ever I had a friend in this world
You've been a friend to me.

Chorus:

My Grandfather's Clock

Here's a song I used to sing in my 4th grade chorus back in elementary school. For some reason it's become a bluegrass standard, especially among banjo players who love to twist their "Scruggs pegs" and play their harmonic "chimes" depicting the old clock that ticked away faithfully until "the old man died".

Since bluegrass musicians rarely sing this, I've kept to the spirit and have written it out as a guitar instrumental. The melody jumps from the bass to the treble, and it should give your picking technique some practice, especially if you have not been into melody picking before. I've indicated pick direction to give you a good feeling for alternate strokes.

If you want to get fancy, I've also written out some harmonics which I think you'll enjoy. In order to get the right sound, simply touch the string lightly directly over the fret indicated and pluck it. You should get a light, bell-like sound.

Under The Double Eagle

Originally a marching band number composed by Josef Franz Wagner in 1903, this tune has become a guitar picker's classic. The version below was transcribed from the playing of Charlie Waller of The Country Gentlemen (*Country Songs, Old and New;* Folkways FA 2409). Waller plays it fairly fast, and double-picks many of the bass notes, which I have not indicated in the TAB for the sake of simplicity.

The first time I ever heard of this tune was on a hitch-hiking trip through upper New York State about 1956. A fellow driving a farm truck drove by and saw me sitting on my guitar case waiting for a ride. He screeched to a stop, jumped out of the cab and yelled at me: "You play that thing?" "Sure do", I yelled back, eager at the prospect of playing some folk music for a Real Folk. "Can you play 'Under The Double Eagle'?" "Nope, I never heard of that one." "Hell, you can't play that thing!" and he roared off, leaving me standing in a cloud of dust.

Rakes Of Mallow

Rakes of Mallow is an old Irish fiddle tune that makes a good guitar, banjo or mandolin piece as well. Many of the best bluegrass and old-time fiddle tunes come from the traditional Irish and Scottish dance music.

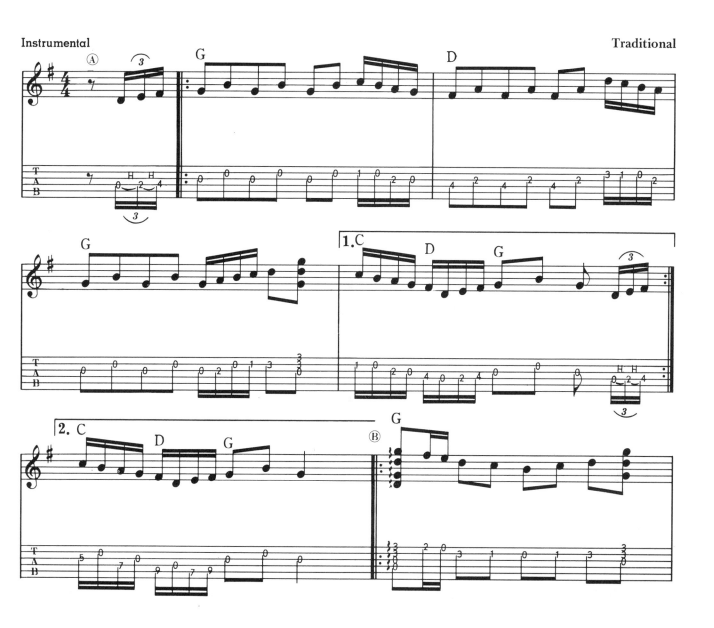

Devil's Dream and Forked Deer

These two fiddle tunes are from the playing of Dan Crary, a favorite guitar soloist among bluegrass enthusiasts. They were transcribed from Dan's excellent American Heritage album called *Bluegrass Guitar* (AHLP-275).

Devil's Dream

Traditional

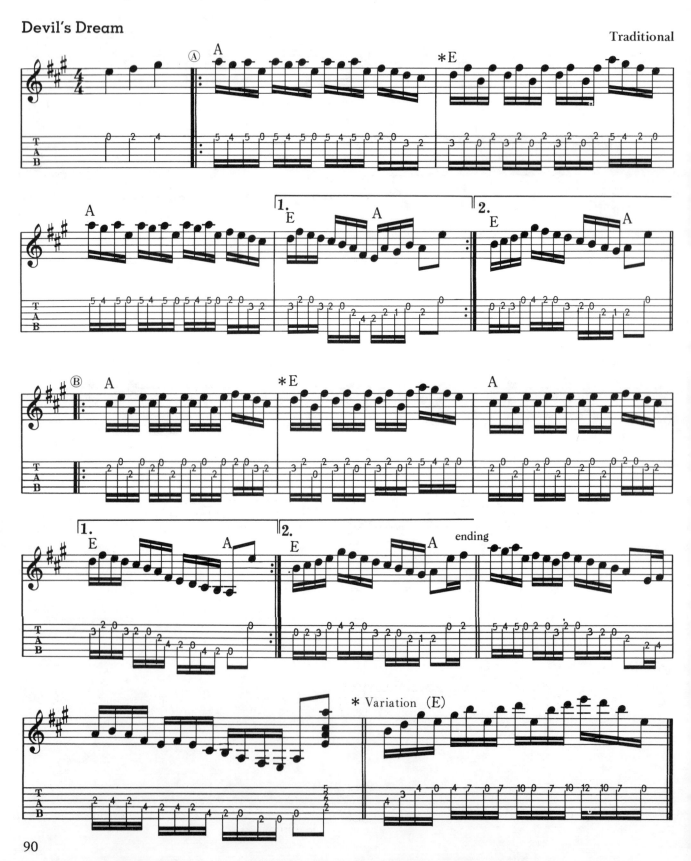

Forked Deer

Actual Key: D
Capo 2nd Fret

Traditional

Forked Deer

Variation:

Soldier's Joy

This is another classic fiddle-banjo-guitar instrumental. As in many of these tunes, the A section is played through twice, and then the B section is played twice (AABB). Get together with a friend and switch off playing the accompaniment and the solo. I've written out a variation for each part to illustrate how you might improvise around the basic melody. After you become familiar with these variations, try some of your own.

Note the double-stops (melody and harmony notes) in the B variation. This is a very useful technique for many kinds of songs.

The Lilly Brothers and Tex Logan

Soldier's Joy

Traditional

John Henry

Here are two instrumental versions of "John Henry". Each has something different to offer, and both will teach you something about solo guitar playing in the bluegrass style.

Try to listen to Clarence White's version on *Appalachian Spring!*, (the Kentucky Colonels —World Pacific 1821).

Newgrass

"Newgrass" is a recently coined expression that describes groups using the traditional bluegrass format to express more contemporary musical viewpoints. A great controversy rages between the traditional bluegrass fans and those who like to see the music take on a more contemporary sound. Proponents of traditional bluegrass are dismayed to see their one-time heros, such as Earl Scruggs and The Osborne Brothers, amplify their instruments and add drums, bringing their music closer to The Byrds than Bill Monroe. These groups, which also include many young, city-bred musicians, often add to their repertoire non-country material, such as Dylan and Beatle songs, or their own original material with a contemporary flavor.

Whatever the merits of the arguments pro and con, one thing is certain. Many excellent musicians are using this format to bring exciting new ideas to bluegrass playing. Although the flat-top acoustic is still the prevalent guitar, there are traces of blues and jazz in many of the more contemporary solos, even in the most traditional tunes.

In the following pages, I have tried to set down some examples of this kind of picking. The solos are difficult, and many of the notes may sound strange until you've got them up to tempo and in the context of the music, so keep at it. Wherever possible, listen carefully to guitarists such as Clarence White, David Bromberg, Jon Sholle, Artie Traum, Randy Scruggs, and others who are playing this style. It will definitely be a challenge to try and play like them!

Jon Sholle

David Bromberg

Orange Mountain Special and Barrel Of Fun

Country Cooking is a good example of a group of young musicians who are keeping bluegrass music fresh and exciting. Using traditional instrumentation and form, the individual soloists are nevertheless unusually inventive.

Both of these solos have been transcribed from the jazz-tinged solos of Russ Barenberg who, like many of the guitarists in this section, has played in several different musical formats, including an electric blues band. On the Country Cooking albums, he emerges as one of the best bluegrass flatpickers around.

"Orange Mountain Special" is from their first album, called *Country Cooking* (Rounder Records 0006) and "Barrel of Fun" is, aptly enough, from *Barrel of Fun* (Rounder 0033).

By the way, Peter Wernick, one of the two banjo players in the group, has written a book called *Bluegrass Banjo,* (Oak) which includes the banjo solos for these two songs. Get together with a friend who picks 5-string and you can start your own Country Cooking.

Country Cooking

Orange Mountain Special

Original Key: A
Capo 2

Peter Wernick
Hank Miller

101

Barrel Of Fun

John M. Miller

Original Key: B
Capo 4

Stoney Creek

This is from the playing of David Nichtern, an excellent guitarist and songwriter in many different musical areas. David writes:

> "Here is a tune called Stoney Creek which I learned from a Jim and Jesse album. The first version is just the melody and the other is an improvisation based on the tune as I would play it if I were sitting around trading solos.

> "Improvisation at its highest (that is to say, least mechanical) level involves the spontaneous creation of a melodic line within the harmonic context (chord changes) of a tune. We should aim at this kind of creation rather than just stringing our 'hot licks' together. We should always carry two flat picks in case we lose one.

> love,
> David Nichtern"

David Nichtern

Stoney Creek

Traditional

Improvisations   Part Ⓐ

Sally Goodin and Arkansas Traveler

Jon Sholle is another excellent guitarist whose work covers a wide range of styles, including bluegrass, jazz, and rock. Here are his arrangements of two well-known fiddle tunes.

Sally Goodin

Traditional

Arkansas Traveler

Traditional

Cross Picking

Cross-picking is a style of flatpicking in which the pick plays the melody note and the surrounding strings in much the same way that bluegrass banjo players do, except that instead of using three fingers, the single flatpick does all the work. This means moving the pick back and forth across the strings with exceptional speed and control, and it will take a lot of concentrated practice to get down. (It should be noted that some guitarists get a similar effect by using the pick in conjunction with their 2nd and 3rd fingers, which means they can switch quickly from fingerpicking to flatpicking.) Doc Watson and Clarence White are the masters of this style. Listen to them!

Before you start, it might help to practice these exercises. Then try "Dill Pickle Rag".

Doc Watson

Dill Pickle Rag

This was originally a ragtime piano tune that has recently become a virtuoso guitar/banjo/mandolin showpiece. You can hear it flatpicked by Doc Watson *(Home Again!,* Vanguard VSD-79239); fingerpicked by Eric Schoenberg and Dave Laibman *(New Ragtime Guitar,* Folkways AHS 3528); bluegrass banjoed by Don Reno *(Another Day,* Reno and Smiley King 816); and cross-picked on mandolin by Jesse McReynolds *(Country Music and Bluegrass at Newport,* Vanguard). I adapted Jesse's version to the guitar, and I think you will enjoy its challenge.

Jim and Jesse

Dill Pickle Rag

115

Sittin' On Top Of The World

This is a very popular song, great for those three and four part bluegrass harmonies.

The instrumental break is from the playing of Artie Traum, and it makes use of some pretty intricate cross-picking. It may sound strange at first, but the faster you play it the better it will sound.

Traditional

Instrumental

Handful Of Love

This bluegrass-type song was written some years back by Artie Traum and was recorded by us on our Capitol album *Double Back* (ST-799). It's an up-tempo, humorous song, and the chords come fast and furious. The instrumental, transcribed from the solo Artie played on the record, is a series of riffs that follow the chord changes but stay pretty much to the same pattern from measure to measure. It's an exciting and challenging break, and I think you'll enjoy playing it. Try to get someone to play rhythm to help you hear the chord changes as you play it.

In the tab you'll notice that some of the numbers are in parenthesis (see measures 7, 8, and 9). This means that the string is depressed at the fret *not* in parenthesis and stretched up until the note reaches the sound it would make at the fret in the parenthesis. In other words, in measure 7, you fret the 2nd string 10th fret (A) and stretch the string until the pitch is raised one whole tone to a B. Get it?

Artie Traum

118

Handful Of Love

Artie Traum

119

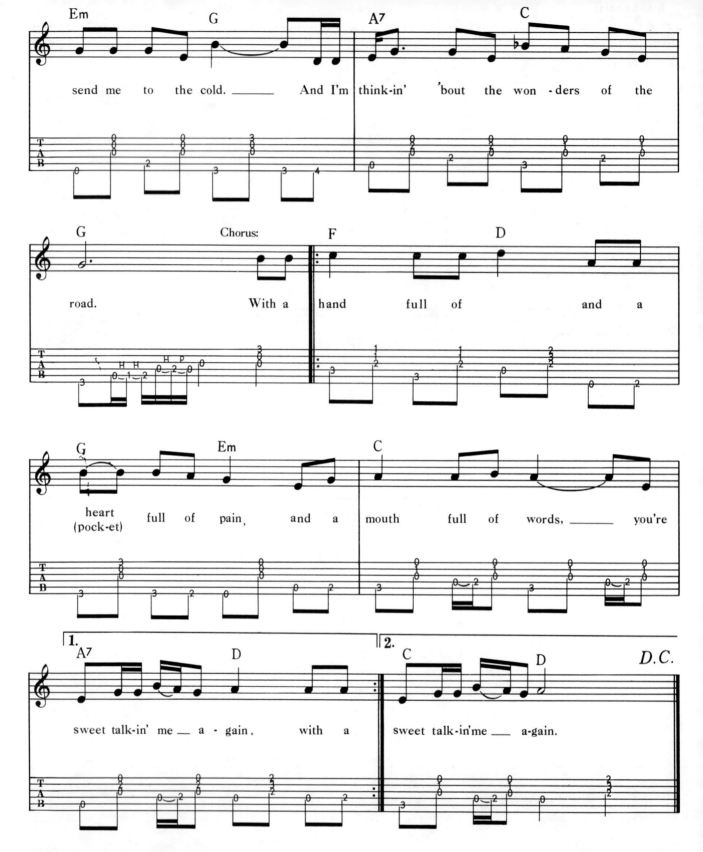

I guess we went too far this time
And over flew our mark
But you didn't know the limits of my soul
And now the tears are passing by and I'm thinkin' 'bout the time
We were oh so young and happy in our home.
(Chorus)

Instrumental

Appendix

Buying a guitar

Choosing a guitar

Most bluegrass guitar players are as traditionally minded about their instruments as they are about the music they are playing. *The* bluegrass guitar is the Martin D-18 or D-28 (the D stands for Dreadnaught), the largest guitar with the deepest, richest tone in the Martin catalogue. Occasionally, a very prosperous musician will own a D-45, which is elaborately decorated with mother-of-pearl inlays and ivory binding, but most are satisfied with any good Martin. The most sought after are the pre-war (World War II) "Herringbones", so called because of the minute inlay patterns which run along the outer contours of the top of the guitar. Pre-war Martins are reputed to have been made with more care, better wood, and have had the time to age and mellow through the years. A good 40-year-old Dreadnaught can fetch as much as $2,500 these days.

The dream of every Martin fancier is to drive through a small town and spot a dingy antique or hock shop with a sign in the window saying, "We Don't Know What We Have". On a wall, or in an old leather case covered with dust, is a beat-up, unstrung guitar with a price tag of $25. On closer inspection, when the grime is wiped away, it is revealed to be a 1936 Martin Herringbone. Unfortunately, it rarely happens. The closest thing to that dream that I have ever seen was the guitar that my brother Artie bought back in 1960. A friend passing through Denver wrote that he saw a pretty good-looking guitar hanging in a store window for $75. Artie needed a guitar but at that time didn't know a herringbone from a tuna fish. Six weeks later a large box arrived in our Bronx apartment containing—yep, a 1936 D-28 Herringbone. You'll see him playing it at any of our concerts. Fifteen years later it's still one of the best guitars I've ever seen.

Another indication of the allure of the old Martin is the incident that occurred not long ago on Matt Umanov's guitar shop in Greenwich Village. Six impeccably dressed Japanese businessmen entered the store and asked for "One pre-war Herringbone, please" in heavily-accented English. They were shown one (which was not for sale) and immediately started writing dimensions and other data in notebooks they took from their attache cases. Watch for a Japanese version very soon!

Other guitars besides Martins are used by bluegrass guitarists, and running a close second is another famous name in American guitars, Gibson. They, too, make an extra-large guitar much beloved by bluegrass pickers, the most respected being the J-200 (J for Jumbo). They also make a Hummingbird model, also widely used, named for the design etched into the pick-guard. The Gibsons have a very different sound and feel than the Martins, and if you are looking for a good guitar, I'd strongly suggest that you play them both and decide which you prefer. Both brands are the top names in steel-string acoustic guitars, and offer a wide variety of styles and prices. Similar to the Gibson in sound and feel is the Guild guitar, which has also developed a strong reputation over the past ten or fifteen years.

Recently, imported guitars have been getting better and better, especially those made in Japan. Yamaha makes a very good imitation of the Martin Dreadnaught, and it costs about half of the real thing. If you are looking to save money, you might investigate some of the dozens of imports that are around. Just remember, as in most things you buy, you usually get what you pay for.

One warning: Whenever you buy a steel string guitar, get a fairly good one. A poorly made guitar will often have a high action, making the instrument difficult to play. Also, unless the neck is reinforced, the pressure of the steel strings can warp the neck or do other damage, so it is worth spending a little extra money and getting an instrument you can really enjoy. A reasonably good steel string acoustic guitar would probably start at about $150.

Where to buy a guitar

A New Guitar. Your best bet is a reputable music store or a department store, if you don't know much about guitars. Just be sure the store gives you a guarantee and the option to return or exchange the instrument for another in case you find it unsuitable. That way, you can show the guitar to a music teacher or a musical friend and get an educated opinion.

A Used Guitar. You can often get an excellent buy on a used guitar, but generally it's more risky than buying a new one. And here, it's requisite that you take someone along with you who really knows guitars. Some music stores handle used as well as new guitars. Other places to check are: classified ads in newspapers, bulletin boards (especially in colleges), thrift shops (not usually a good source, but worth a try), and pawn shops.*

What details to check for

Action. The action of a guitar is the distance between the string and the fingerboard. A high action—that is, too great a distance—makes it difficult to press the strings down. But a low action—too small a distance,—may cause the strings to buzz and the tone to be impaired. A good guitar should have a fairly even action from one end of the fingerboard to the other, with the strings never more than 1/8 of an inch from the fingerboard.

Frets. The pitch of the guitar is based on the accuracy of the frets which are placed with mathematical precision. Anyone with a musical ear will be able to tell if they're off even the slightest bit. Various defects can be responsible for the frets being out of tune: improper placement, a warped neck, or an inaccurately placed bridge.

You can check your frets in the following way. Play an open string and listen carefully to its pitch. Then fret the same string on the twelfth fret and pluck again. This note should be exactly one octave higher than the first. Repeat this procedure with each string. If every octave is true, you can be fairly certain your frets are accurate. Here's another test you can try. Make sure your guitar is perfectly in tune. Then play a full six-string chord, and fret it at each fret along the fingerboard. Listen carefully to each string. If the chord sounds out of tune at any point, something is probably wrong with the frets.

Pickguards. Most guitars come with plastic or tortoise shell pickguards to protect the finish from being scratched. If your guitar doesn't have one a guitar repairman can put one on for you.

---

*It was once possible to make the rounds of the pawn shops in a big city and come across a great buy in a used guitar. This isn't the case anymore. Pawn shop dealers have become more sophisticated about the value of used guitars since the folk and rock 'n' roll "booms" and the soaring popularity of the guitar. It's still possible to come across a good guitar in a pawn shop, and sometimes you can get a good price on it, but this is becoming increasingly rare. Many pawn shops now deal in new instruments—usually of inferior quality—which they hang in the window with "Sale" signs all over them.

Stringing your guitar

After several weeks of playing, you'll notice that the strings on your guitar are showing signs of wear. They'll be difficult to keep in tune and will sound somewhat dull. The guitar might not sound "true" at all the frets; that is, it will sound out of tune when fretted up the neck, even though it's in tune when placed in the open positions. Nylon strings tend to fray or unravel, and steel strings develop indentations from the constant pressure of the frets.

All stringed instruments are based on the same principle. The string is fixed at one end to the bridge or tailpiece and wrapped around the movable tuning peg on the other. But there are differences in the way you string the steel and the nylon string guitar.

Steel string guitars have either a tailpiece or a bridge with small round holes going through it and into the body of the guitar, with bridge pins that fit in the hole over the string. Steel strings are made with a "ball end," a small metal piece that catches in the bridge or tailpiece and holds the string fast. You then put the straight end of the string through the hole in the tuning shaft and tighten the string to pitch.

The unwound treble strings have a tendency to slip as they're being tuned. To prevent this, wind the string on top of itself a couple of times. Then when it's tuned it will catch on the shaft and hold fast. Wind all the strings in the same direction, usually counterclockwise. Leave enough slack in the string so you can wrap it around the tuning shaft at least three times when you tune it up to pitch. After the string is tuned, clip off the excess wire.

Steel strings tend to sound harsh and metallic at first. But they'll break in after a few hours of playing and sound more mellow and pleasant.

Type of strings

Steel strings come in different gauges or thicknesses—heavy, medium, light, and extra light. The type you use will depend on your guitar, your hand strength, and the sound you're after. Most bluegrass rhythm guitarists like heavy gauge strings and a fairly high action, to give them that fat, booming bass sound. The medium gauge strings are more versatile, and it is not as difficult to play fast lead solos on them. Unless you are playing primarily lead guitar, you probably won't want light gauge strings for bluegrass playing. They don't provide a solid enough sound to give the rest of the band the support they need from the guitarist. Only you, ultimately, can tell what you want to play on, so experiment until you find the gauge and brand of strings that you like.

Caring for your guitar

The better the care you give a guitar, the longer it will last—and the better it will sound. So here are some tips on how to treat your guitar.

Avoid drastic changes in temperature and humidity. Keep your guitar away from radiators, steam pipes, and other sources of heat in the house. Don't leave it out in the sun or in the cold for any length of time. Although a well-made instrument can take a certain amount of climate change, cracking, warping or glue-separation may occur as a result of drastic changes.

Clean the face of the guitar from time to time, since a film of dirt and perspiration usually develops on it and can eventually become ingrained in the finish. You can do the job with a slightly dampened cloth most of the time, but once in a while use some guitar polish to clean the wood thoroughly and give it a high luster. Remember, too, to wipe off the fretboard everytime you finish playing. This helps preserve the life of the strings, since perspiration can corrode the metal strings.

Keep your guitar tuned to standard pitch. Check it occasionally with a piano, pitchpipe, or tuning fork. If you tune it too high it might result in a warped neck or a loosened bridge.

Keep your guitar in its case when it's not in use. This will avert accidents. If you leave it leaning against a wall it might get kicked over and if you leave it lying around on a chair, sofa or bed, it might get sat on.

Have cracks repaired immediately otherwise they'll get larger and might lead to other damage. Even the finest guitars can crack, either from a change in temperature which causes the wood to expand or contract, or from a blow to the thin top or back. A cracked guitar isn't a very serious matter if you take care of it at once. An experienced repairman can fix it without any damage to its tone or playability.

Replace tuning pegs when necessary. After a few years, the gears on the tuning pegs might wear out, causing them to slip. Or the knob might become damaged in some way. Pegs can be purchased easily in any large music center.

Trouble shooting

There are many reasons why you might get string buzz on your guitar. Some you can handle yourself and some will make it necessary to bring the instrument to a repairman. Here's a list of the most common causes of string buzz and what to do about them:

You may be fretting the string improperly. Your finger should be pressing the string firmly to the fingerboard, as close to the fret as you can get without actually touching it.

One or more of the frets might be too high. A repairman can easily file or replace the fret wire in this case.

The action may be too low. You can correct this either by raising the bridge or the nut, or by adjusting the truss rod in a steel string guitar.

There may be a warp or "hump" in the neck. This isn't easy to correct, but a good repairman can straighten a warped fingerboard.

The strings may not be tuned up to pitch. This causes them to vibrate too widely and hit the fingerboard.

The bridge or nut might need adjusting. Most likely you'll need to take this job to a repairman.

Hearing live bluegrass

As far as I am concerned, the best way to hear any kind of music is in live performance. Fortunately, there are opportunities in almost every part of the country to hear bluegrass in concerts, night clubs, state fairs, and especially festivals. One of the nicest things about bluegrass musicians is their attitude towards their fans—an almost universal feeling of pride in meeting and playing for "the folks", recognizing that these people have been responsible for their success. With very few exceptions, this attitude prevails even among the most well known and successful bluegrass stars.

The festivals are the most popular source of live bluegrass today, and have been proliferating at an incredible rate all over the country. The April, 1974 issue of *Pickin'* for instance, lists 115 different festivals for that year. The other leading magazines, such as *Muleskinner News* and *Bluegrass Unlimited,* also publish schedules of events across the country, including bluegrass festivals, old-time fiddler's conventions, and other folk and country music festivals. There are many reasons that these festivals have become so popular, among them the fact that one can see and hear dozens of groups from all over the country during the course of a weekend. But I think the main attraction is relaxed informality of the atmosphere, and if a festival is produced well it is sometimes possible to see and speak with performers that might otherwise be heard only on records, or from the distant balcony of a concert hall. At the smaller festivals, especially, it is even possible to jam with a well-known picker and really learn something about the music first hand.

Publications

As with festivals, the number of bluegrass magazines are growing too, and some of them are chock full of all kinds of information. *Bluegrass Unlimited* (Box 111, Burke, Virginia 22015) and *Muleskinner News* (Rt. 2, Box 304, Elon College, N.C. 27244) have been printing articles, interviews, record reviews, gossip, and occasional instruction material for a number of years now, and are the best-known and most consistent magazines in the field. They are strictly bluegrass publications, and do not deal with any other kinds of music. *Pickin'* (1 Saddle Road, Cedar Knolls, N.J. 07927) is a slick new magazine dedicated to both bluegrass and old-time country music. Although it has been out only a short time as of this writing, it shows a lot of promise, and hopefully will take its place with the others as a permanent part of the bluegrass scene.

Many other publications deal with bluegrass music, but not exclusively. My favorite, of course, *Sing Out! The Folk Song Magazine* (106 West 28 Street N.Y.C. 10001) has published many bluegrass songs and articles during its 24 years of publication, as well as every other aspect of rural and urban folk music. *Guitar Player* (348 No. Santa Cruz, Los Gatos, Ca. 95030) has articles on the guitar ranging from folk to rock to jazz, and occasionally has articles on bluegrass performers. This magazine is interesting for its general information about the guitar, which is useful no matter what kind of music you like to play.

Recordings

The field of bluegrass music on record is so vast that it would be impossible to compile a complete list of available records. However, it might aid your approach to bluegrass on record if I list those albums that were especially useful to me in preparing this book, and also some of my personal favorites. These records were chosen, with the help of friends such as Bill Keith and Eric Weissberg, for the strong guitar work and general excellence of playing. This should not be taken as a definitive discography, though, and I'm sure that there are many deserving records that have been left out. Keep your eyes and ears open, and I'm sure you'll quickly add to this list.

Old-Time and Early Bluegrass

Early Blue Grass RCA Vintage Series LPV-569. Old recordings of The Morris Brothers, The Monroe Brothers, Jimmy Martin, and others.

Early Blue Grass Music By The Monroe Brothers RCA Camden CAL-774. Twelve reissued sides, not a bad one in the bunch.
The Delmore Brothers Country 402. Lots of fine guitar picking. An absolute favorite of mine.
Old-Time Southern Dance Music—The String Bands Old-Timey Records. Pre-bluegrass anthology of string bands, this is a dynamic record with Charlie Poole, Hackberry Ramblers, Arthur Smith Trio, and others. Available from Box 5073, Berkeley, California.

The Carter Family
Recordings by The Carter Family are essential to an understanding of early bluegrass guitar style. There are many reissues out, among them: *Country Sounds of The Original Carter Family* Harmony/Columbia HL 7422
Great Original Recordings by The Carter Family HL 7300
Great Sacred Songs HL 7396

Doc Watson
Doc Watson, while not a bluegrass musician in the true sense of the word, has been so influential to the bluegrass guitar scene that he must be mentioned here. His earliest records are still my favorites:
Old Time Music at Clarence Ashley's Folkways FA 2355 and (Part 2)—FA 2359
The Watson Family FA 2366. Doc has also made several records for Vanguard, all of which are highly recommended.

Bluegrass

Bill Monroe

The Father of Blue Grass Music RCA Camden CAL-719. A collection of classic performances, recorded in the early 1940's, including "Six White Horses", "Mule Skinner Blues", and other Monroe standards.
The High Lonesome Sound of Bill Monroe and His Blue Grass Boys Decca DL 74780. A collection from the early 50's with a variety of guitarists including Jimmy Martin, Eddie Mayfield, and Carter Stanley!
The Great Bill Monroe Harmony/Columbia HL 7290.
Blue Grass Time Decca DL 74896. Recorded in the mid-60's with young city bluegrass musicians, such as Bill Keith, banjo; Richard Greene, fiddle; and Peter Rowan on guitar. Del McCoury plays guitar on some cuts too.

Don Reno and Red Smiley
Country Songs King 701. This record, more than any other that I have heard, shows off Don Reno's

excellent guitar style, and his duets with Red Smiley are memorable. Most of their other records, listed below, emphasize Reno's banjo.

Instrumentals by Don Reno and Red Smiley and The Tennessee Cutups—King 552.

Country Singing & Instrumentals King 776. Some fine picking, including a nice version of "Double Eagle".

Another Day King 816. Banjo versions of "Dill Pickles" and "Grandfather's Clock", but not much guitar.

The Stanley Brothers

This is my personal favorite bluegrass group, partly because of the richness of their harmonies and the obviously traditional roots of their music, but also because of the strong use of lead guitar on almost all their songs. Here are a few of their records:

The Stanley Brothers and The Clinch Mountain Boys Sing The Songs They Like Best King 772.

Country Pickin' and Singin' Mercury MG 20349.

Stanley Brothers and the Clinch Mountain Boys King 615.

Everybody's Country Favorites King 690. In my opinion, this is the best of The Stanley Brothers. Judge for yourself.

Ralph Stanley: Something Old—Something New Rebel SLP-1503. Recorded after the death of Carter Stanley, this brings Ralph's music up to date with some fine picking and singing, including one Jesse Winchester song—in the bluegrass style, of course.

Jimmy Martin

Jimmy Martin and his Sunny Mountain Boys have been bluegrass favorites for nearly 25 years. Two of my favorites are:

Widow Maker Decca DL 74536.

Country Music Time Decca DL 74285.

Lester Flatt and Earl Scruggs

Any of the fine Flatt and Scruggs albums on Columbia will be important contributions to your bluegrass collection. Very few feature lead guitar, although Earl Scruggs occasionally switches to guitar on some songs. When he does, he usually plays in a fingerpicking style. Here are some of their best albums:

Foggy Mountain Jamboree Columbia CL 1019.

Country Music Mercury MG 20358.

Songs of Glory Columbia CL 1424.

The World of Flatt and Scruggs Columbia KG 31964 (A two-record set.).

Clarence White

Unfortunately, the number of bluegrass recordings made by Clarence before his death were relatively few, but they are essential to anyone interested in great guitar picking. I have not listed his work with rock groups such as the Byrds, since their music does not fall within the framework of this book.

Appalachian Swing! The Kentucky Colonels World Pacific 1821. Twelve incredible instrumentals. A must!

Bluegrass America—The Kentucky Colonels Briar International M109

Dobro Country (Tut Taylor) World Pacific 1829. Excellent dobro picking by Tut Taylor with Clarence playing back-up guitar.

New Dimensions in Banjo & Bluegrass (Recently reissued as *Dueling Banjos;* the theme music from *Deliverance* Elektra/Warner Bros. Great banjo picking by Eric Weissberg and Marshall Brickman, with Clarence White on guitar. Clarence plays some excellent solos, as well as his usual solid back-up.

The Country Gentlemen

These records by one of the most popular "younger" bluegrass bands (they've only been playing since the late 50's) features Charlie Waller on guitar. You'll learn a great deal from his back-up style.

The Country Gentlemen Sing and Play Folk Songs and Bluegrass Folkways FA 2410.

Country Songs—Old and New Folkways FA 2409.

Folk Session Inside Mercury MG 20858.

Dan Crary

The only record of Dan Crary's fine picking that I know of is *Bluegrass Guitar* American Heritage 27S (912 North 8th St. Boise, Idaho 83702).

The Greenbriar Boys

The best of the city folk/bluegrass groups features John Herald's excellent flatpicking and lead singing.

The Greenbriar Boys Vanguard VRS-9104.

Ragged But Right VRS-9159.

Better Late Than Never! VRS-9233.

Country Cooking

An instrumental group with guitar picking by Russ Barenberg and five other excellent young players. Their records are inventive and exciting.

Country Cooking Rounder 0006.

Barrel of Fun Rounder 0033.

Miscellaneous

Will The Circle Be Unbroken United Artists 9801. A three-record set with many of the most important figures in the world of bluegrass and country music jamming together. Brought together by The Nitty Gritty Dirt Band, this record will always be a classic. Don't miss it!

Del McCoury Sings Bluegrass Arhoolie F 5006. McCoury's powerful tenor voice and solid flatpick back-up make this a fine album.

Mud Acres—Music Among Friends Rounder

3001. Not strictly a bluegrass album, it nevertheless features Jim Rooney and Bill Keith, John Herald, Maria Muldaur, and Happy and Artie Traum in some folk/country classics. I like it.

Other groups that you might enjoy are:
The Seldom Scene; The Dillards; J.D. Crowe; The Newgrass Revival; Country Gazette, Breakfast Special, and The New Shades of Grass, to mention just a few of the fine groups working the bluegrass circuit. My apologies to those I have left out.

If you live in an area in which it is difficult to find good bluegrass records, there is a fast-growing trend towards mail-order book and record sales. The bluegrass magazines (see above) are filled with ads for small record companies selling their product by mail. A good idea, I think, since small companies can by-pass the large record distributors, who tend to be interested mainly in the best-selling hot item of the day. In the folk, country, and bluegrass fields, it is these small, independent labels, such as Folkways, Rounder, County, Philo, Folk Legacy, Arhoolie, etc. who are often putting out the best music, so if you are interested, check out the mail order business.

There are two mail order distributors who are currently handling an enormous number of hard-to-get records, and at reasonable prices. They are: Rounder Sales, 186 Willow Ave. Somerville, Mass. 02143; and County Sales, 307 East 37th St. New York City 10016. Write to them for their catalogues.

If you are interested in pursuing your guitar studies further, I have several series of guitar lessons on tapes and cassettes, covering just about every aspect of folk, bluegrass, and rock guitar. You can write me at Homespun Tapes, Box 694, Woodstock, N.Y. 12498 for all the information.

← A   Tape here

— —

Cut

To make a convenient holder for your sound sheet, cut along the inside edge
of the page with a razor or knife from the dotted line to the bottom of the
page. Fold up the bottom section at the dotted line and tape at point A.